AF228982

Lerner SPORTS

GREATEST OF ALL TIME PLAYERS

G.O.A.T. HOCKEY GOALIES

Josh Anderson

Lerner Publications ◆ Minneapolis

Lerner Publications Company
An imprint of Lerner Publishing Group, Inc.
241 First Avenue North
Minneapolis, MN 55401 USA

For reading levels and more information, look up this title at www.lernerbooks.com.

Main body text set in Aptifer Sans LT Pro.
Typeface provided by Linotype AG.

Library of Congress Cataloging-in-Publication Data

Names: Anderson, Josh, author.
Title: G.O.A.T. hockey goalies / Josh Anderson.
Other titles: Greatest of all time hockey goalies
Description: Minneapolis. MN : Lerner Publications , [2024] | Series: Lerner sports. Greatest of all time players | Includes bibliographical references and index. | Audience: Ages 7–11 | Audience: Grades 2–3 | Summary: "Few positions in sports are more important than the hockey goalie. Learn about the greatest goalies in hockey history, explore their impact on the game, and then create your own list of the G.O.A.T. goalies"— Provided by publisher.
Identifiers: LCCN 2023018040 (print) | LCCN 2023018041 (ebook) | ISBN 9798765610244 (library binding) | ISBN 9798765623633 (paperback) | ISBN 9798765614983 (epub)
Subjects: LCSH: Hockey players—Canada—Biography—Juvenile literature. | Hockey players—United States—Juvenile literature. | Hockey goalkeepers—Biography—Juvenile literature. | BISAC: JUVENILE NONFICTION / Biography & Autobiography / Sports & Recreation
Classification: LCC GV848.5.A1 A644 2024 (print) | LCC GV848.5.A1 (ebook) | DDC 796.962092/2—dc23/eng/20230420

LC record available at https://lccn.loc.gov/2023018040
LC ebook record available at https://lccn.loc.gov/2023018041

Manufactured in the United States of America
1 – CG – 12/15/23

TABLE OF CONTENTS

Dominik Hašek *(center right)* protects the goal in a game against the Philadelphia Flyers in 1998.

AN INCREDIBLE SAVE

Many great hockey moments are incredible passes that lead to goals. Others are powerful shots that fly past the goalie and into the net. But some goalies are skilled enough to create their own amazing highlights.

The Buffalo Sabres and Philadelphia Flyers were tied 1–1 late in the 1997–1998 National Hockey League (NHL) season. Philadelphia's all-star center, Eric Lindros, skated toward Buffalo's goal. Sabres goalie Dominik Hašek was ready.

FACTS AT A GLANCE

» **MARTIN BRODEUR** IS THE ALL-TIME NHL SAVES LEADER WITH 28,928.

» **VLADISLAV TRETIAK** NEVER PLAYED IN THE NHL, BUT HE IS STILL ONE OF THE BEST GOALIES OF ALL TIME.

» **DOMINIK HAŠEK** RANKS THIRD ALL-TIME IN THE NHL WITH A .922 SAVE PERCENTAGE.

» **SHANNON SZABADOS** WAS THE FIRST WOMAN TO EVER PLAY IN THE SOUTHERN PROFESSIONAL HOCKEY LEAGUE.

Lindros attacked from the right side. Hašek moved to block a shot from Lindros. But at the last moment, Lindros passed the puck toward the left side of the goal. Flyers right wing Trent Klatt took the pass. He tapped the puck toward the open goal on Hašek's other side.

Hašek didn't have time to fully turn his body and use his stick for a save. Instead, he dropped his

Eric Lindros

stick to the ice and dove toward the puck. He hit it with his blocker, the glove he used to hold his stick. The puck skidded past the goal and safely to the side. Hašek's save was a key moment in the 2–1 Buffalo victory, and one of the greatest of his career.

Hašek focuses on the puck, ready to make a save.

When it comes to goalies, was Hašek the greatest of all time (G.O.A.T.)? Or does that honor belong to another superstar goalie? Let's find out!

Shannon Szabados has often been the first woman to play in hockey tournaments and leagues that were usually made up of only men. She was the first woman to play in the Western Hockey League, the Alberta Junior Hockey League, and the Southern Professional Hockey League.

Szabados led Canada to Olympic Games gold medals in 2010 and 2014. Before the 2010 Olympics in Vancouver, Canada, Team Canada coaches expected Szabados to be one of the team's backup goalies. But she was so good in the games before the Olympics that she earned her place as the team's top goalie. Szabados had two shutouts in the 2010 Olympics and was on the tournament's all-star team.

At the 2014 Olympics in Sochi, Russia, Team Canada won all three of the games Szabados started, including the gold medal game. Canada finished with the silver medal at the 2018 Olympics in PyeongChang, South Korea, and Szabados was named best goalie of the Games. *Women's Hockey Life* named Szabados Player of the Decade in 2019.

SHANNON SZABADOS STATS

Save Percentage	.949
Goals Against Average	1.2
World Championship Gold Medals	1
Olympic Gold Medals	2

Save percentage and goals against average are from the 2018 Olympic Games.

VLADISLAV TRETIAK

Vladislav Tretiak never played in the NHL. The Montréal Canadiens drafted him in 1983, but the Russian government would not allow him to join the team. Fans around the world still know Tretiak was one of the greatest goalies of all time.

Tretiak helped lead Russia to 10 World Championships and three Olympic gold medals. Tretiak played in only one

Olympics where Russia failed to win the gold medal. Team USA defeated Team Russia at the 1980 Olympics in Lake Placid, New York. Fans call this game the Miracle on Ice because Team USA was not expected to beat Tretiak and the Russians.

As a pro, Tretiak led his teams to 13 championships in the Soviet League. In 2008, he became one of six players on the International Ice Hockey Federation Centennial All-Star team. This list honored the best players of the past 100 years. Tretiak is also a member of the Hockey Hall of Fame.

VLADISLAV TRETIAK STATS

Goals Against Average	1.78
Olympic Gold Medals	3
World Championship Gold Medals	10
Soviet League Championships	13

Goals against average is from play with Team Russia.

GRANT FUHR

Hall of Famer Grant Fuhr played for six teams during his NHL career. He spent 10 of his 19 seasons with the Edmonton Oilers. He helped lead the team to four Stanley Cup titles during the 1980s.

When the NHL named its top 100 players of all time, the league included Fuhr. He led the NHL in wins and saves twice. Fuhr's 403 wins rank 12th in NHL history. He holds the NHL record for most assists in a single season by a goalie with 14 in 1983–1984. Fuhr also led the NHL with four shutouts during the 1987–1988 season.

Fuhr was the first Black player to win a Stanley Cup and the first Black player chosen for Hockey's Hall of Fame. He was a teammate of hockey legend Wayne Gretzky for seven seasons. Gretzky has called Fuhr the greatest goalie in NHL history.

GRANT FUHR STATS

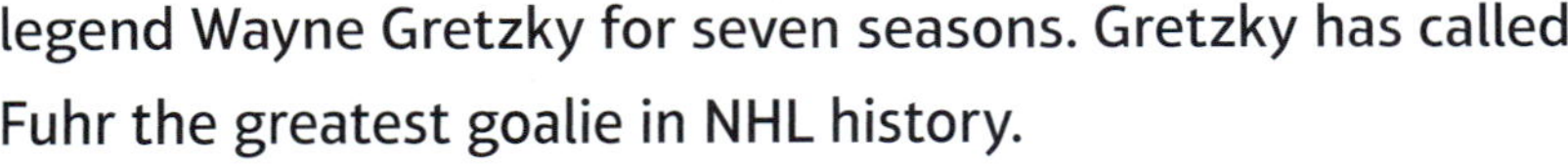

Save Percentage	.887
Goals Against Average	3.38
Wins	403
NHL All-Star Games	6

KEN DRYDEN

Ken Dryden led the Montréal Canadiens to six Stanley Cup wins in his eight seasons in the NHL. He ranks fourth all-time with a .922 save percentage. And he ranks eighth in NHL history with a 2.24 goals against average.

Dryden won the Vezina Trophy as the NHL's top goalie five times. When the NHL chose its top 100 players of all time in 2017, Dryden was included. Dryden's brother Dave Dryden was also an NHL goalie. They are the only brothers to play against each other as goalies in NHL history.

Hall of Famer Ken Dryden's career was shorter than the careers of many other hockey legends. He took a season off to earn his law degree. Then he retired after his eighth season to focus on his law career. From 2004 to 2011, he served in Canada's parliament, the country's main lawmaking body.

KEN DRYDEN STATS

Save Percentage	.922
Goals Against Average	2.24
Wins	258
NHL All-Star Games	5

GLENN HALL

Glenn Hall's nickname was Mr. Goalie because he was the NHL's best goalie of the 1950s and 1960s. Hall played 10 of his 18 seasons for the Chicago Blackhawks. In 1961, he helped lead Chicago to its first Stanley Cup win since 1938.

Hall led the NHL in wins four times, goals against three times, and saves twice. He holds the NHL goalie record with

502 games started in a row. Hall ranks sixth all-time with 24,611 saves. And he won the Vezina Trophy as the league's best goalie three times.

Hall helped start a new style that NHL goalies still use. He was one of the earliest goalies to use the butterfly style. A butterfly goalie protects the goal by dropping to their knees and spreading their hands in a single movement. The style looks similar to the movement of a butterfly. In 2017, the NHL named Hall one of its top 100 players of all time. He is also a member of the Hockey Hall of Fame.

GLENN HALL STATS

Save Percentage	.918
Goals Against Average	2.50
Wins	407
NHL All-Star Games	13

JACQUES PLANTE

Hall of Famer Jacques Plante played 11 of his 18 seasons with the Montréal Canadiens. He led the team to six Stanley Cup titles. Plante won the Hart Memorial Trophy in 1962 as the NHL's MVP. He is one of only seven goalies to win this award. Plante also won the Vezina Trophy as the league's best goalie seven times.

Plante is one of the NHL's top 100 players of all time and ranks near the top in many stats. He is fifth all-time with 82 career shutouts, seventh with a .920 save percentage, and ninth in wins with 437.

But Plante's biggest impact on the NHL was not a save or a win. After a puck hit him in the face and caused a major injury, Plante became the first goalie to regularly wear a mask during games. In the modern NHL, all goalies wear helmets and masks. This practice has cut down on serious head and face injuries.

JACQUES PLANTE STATS

Save Percentage	.920
Goals Against Average	2.38
Wins	437
NHL All-Star Games	8

TERRY SAWCHUK

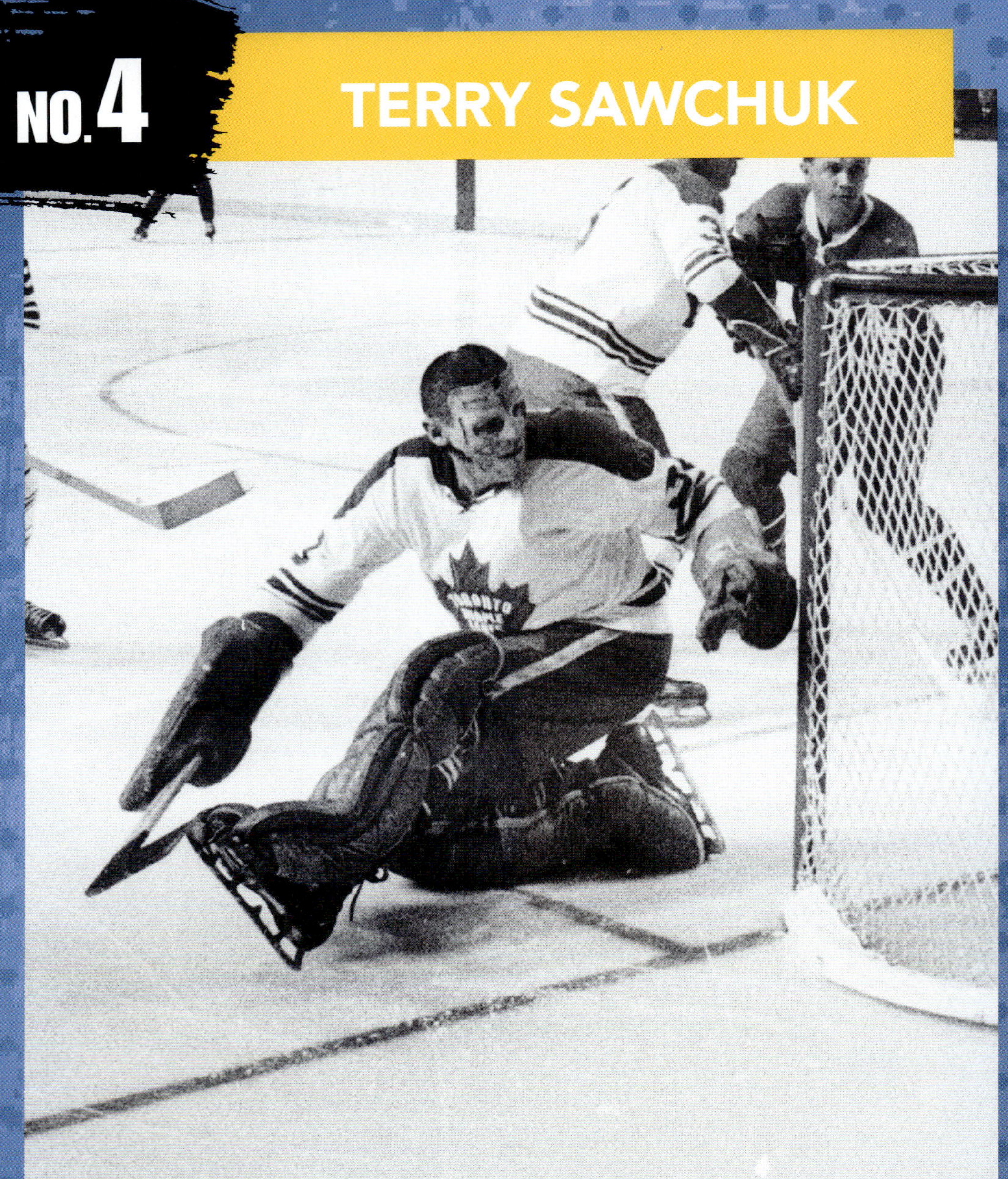

Terry Sawchuk helped lead his teams to four Stanley Cup titles. He played 21 seasons in the NHL, including 14 with the Detroit Red Wings. He led the NHL in wins five seasons in a row from 1950–1951 through 1954–1955.

Named by the NHL as one of its top 100 players of all time, Sawchuk won the Vezina Trophy as the NHL's best goalie four times. He led the league in shutouts three times and goals against average twice. He ranks eighth all-time with 445 career wins and second all-time with 103 shutouts. He was the all-time leader in both wins and shutouts when he retired in 1970. Sawchuk held the career shutout record for 39 years until Martin Brodeur broke it in 2009.

Sawchuck joined the Hockey Hall of Fame in 1971. He also won the Lester Patrick Trophy that year for his impact on hockey in the United States.

TERRY SAWCHUK STATS

Save Percentage	.907
Goals Against Average	2.50
Wins	445
NHL All-Star Games	11

PATRICK ROY

Patrick Roy played for the Montréal Canadiens and Colorado Avalanche during his 19-year NHL career. He led each team to two Stanley Cup titles. Roy won the Conn Smythe Trophy as MVP of the NHL playoffs in 1985–1986, 1992–1993, and 2000–2001.

Roy ranks second all-time with 551 career wins. His 25,800 saves are third in NHL history. He led the league in save percentage four times, goals against average three times, and shutouts three times. The Hall of Famer won the Vezina Trophy as the league's best goalie three times.

The NHL chose Roy as one of its top 100 players of all time in 2017. While many goalies had used the butterfly style before, Roy's success helped make it the most common goalie style in modern hockey. He was a coach in Canada's junior league from 2005 until 2023. He also coached in the NHL from 2013 to 2016.

PATRICK ROY STATS

Save Percentage	.910
Goals Against Average	2.54
Wins	551
NHL All-Star Games	11

DOMINIK HAŠEK

Dominik Hašek played in 16 NHL seasons, mostly with the Buffalo Sabres and Detroit Red Wings. Hašek helped lead Detroit to two Stanley Cup titles.

One of the top 100 players in NHL history, Hašek ranks third all-time with a .922 career save percentage. He led the league in save percentage six times in a row from 1993–1994 to 1998–1999. His 2.20 goals against average rank seventh all-time. He led the league in shutouts four times and goals against average twice. Hašek won the Vezina Trophy as the NHL's best goalie six times.

His strong play and first name led to Hašek's nickname, the Dominator. The Hall of Famer is the only goalie to win the Hart Memorial Trophy as the NHL's MVP twice. In 1998, he led the Czech Republic to its first and only Olympic gold medal in ice hockey.

DOMINIK HAŠEK STATS

Save Percentage	.922
Goals Against Average	2.20
Wins	389
NHL All-Star Games	6

MARTIN BRODEUR

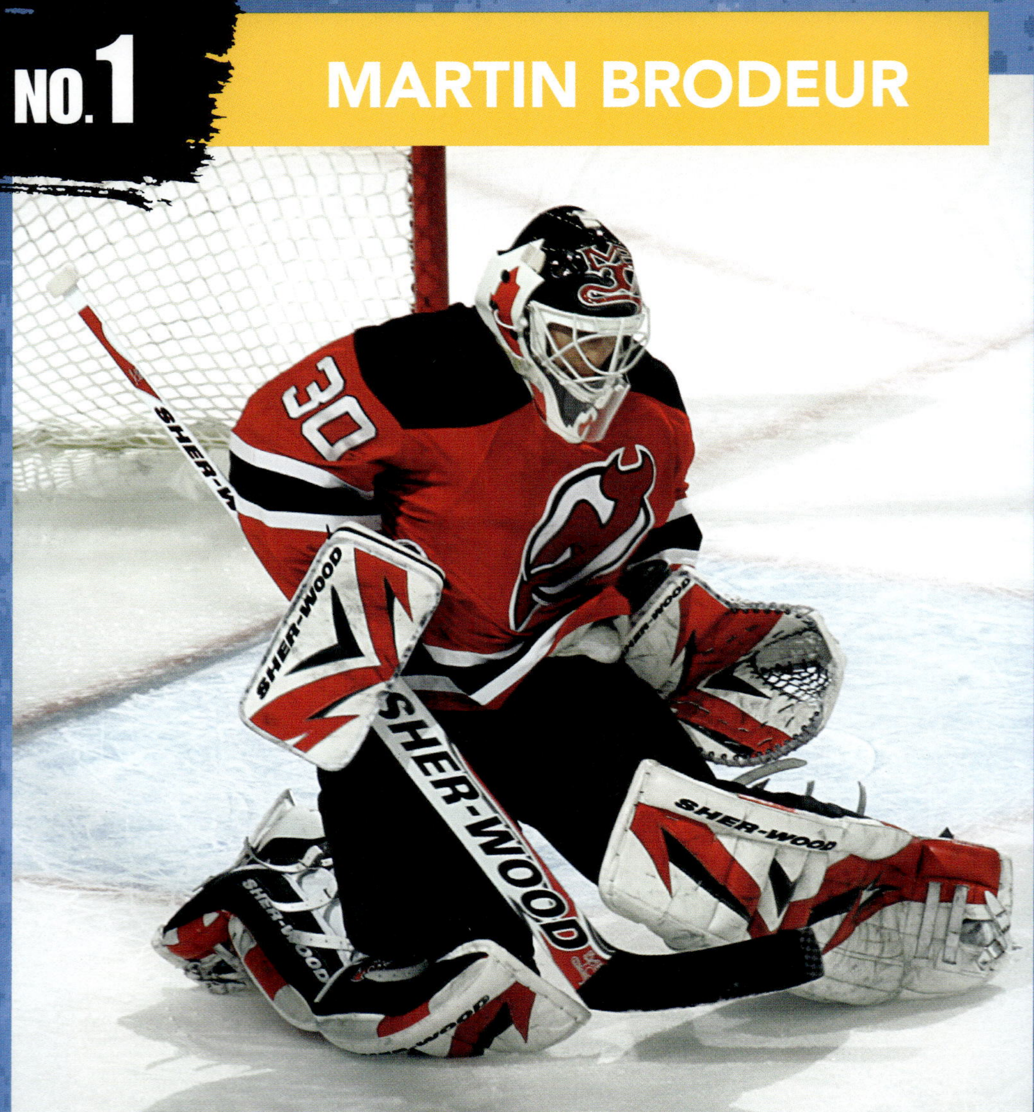

Martin Brodeur played in the NHL from 1992 to 2015. He spent 21 seasons with the New Jersey Devils. Brodeur led the Devils to the only three Stanley Cup titles in team history.

Brodeur ranks first all-time with 691 wins. He's also the NHL's career leader in saves with 28,928 and shutouts with

125. He led the NHL in wins nine times. Brodeur is the only goalie in history with eight seasons of at least 40 wins. He won the Vezina Trophy as the league's best goalie four times.

Brodeur is one of only 12 goalies to ever score a goal in an NHL regular season game. He did it three times. Brodeur won two Olympic gold medals as Team Canada's goalie in 2002 and 2010. In 2017, the NHL listed the Hall of Famer as one of its top 100 players of all time. Brodeur retired after the 2014–2015 season. He later returned to the Devils to help the team choose players and make other important decisions.

MARTIN BRODEUR STATS

Save Percentage	.912
Goals Against Average	2.24
Wins	691
NHL All-Star Games	9

EVEN MORE G.O.A.T.

There have been so many amazing goalies throughout hockey history. Choosing only 10 is a challenge. Here are 10 others who could have made the G.O.A.T. list.

No. 11	JOHNNY BOWER
No. 12	NOORA RÄTY
No. 13	TONY ESPOSITO
No. 14	BERNIE PARENT
No. 15	CLINT BENEDICT
No. 16	GEORGES VÉZINA
No. 17	ROBERTO LUONGO
No. 18	KIM ST-PIERRE
No. 19	ED BELFOUR
No. 20	FRANK BRIMSEK

YOUR G.O.A.T.

It's your turn to make a goalie G.O.A.T. list. If some of your favorite players don't play goalie, make a list for another position too! You can also make G.O.A.T. lists for movies, books, and other things you like.

Start by doing research. You can check out the Learn More section on page 31. The books and websites listed there will help you learn more about hockey players of the past and present. You can also search online for even more information about great players.

Once you have your list, ask friends or family to create a list too. Compare them and see how they differ. Did your friends' lists make you reconsider your own? Talk it over and decide whose G.O.A.T. list is your favorite.

GLOSSARY

backup: a person who takes the place of or supports another

goals against average: a stat that measures how many goals a goalie gives up in a normal game

Hall of Famer: a player who is honored at the Hockey Hall of Fame in Toronto, Canada

MVP: short for *most valuable player*

pro: short for *professional*, taking part in an activity to make money

save: a play that stops the other team from scoring

save percentage: a stat that measures how often a goalie blocks shots that would have scored

shutout: a game in which one team fails to score

Stanley Cup: the NHL's championship trophy

start: to be in the lineup at the beginning of a game

win: a stat that measures how often a goalie was on the ice when their team's winning goal was scored

LEARN MORE

Britannica Kids—Ice Hockey
https://kids.britannica.com/kids/article/Ice-Hockey/353257

Doeden, Matt. *G.O.A.T. Hockey Teams*. Minneapolis: Lerner Publications, 2021.

Fishman, Jon M. *Hockey's G.O.A.T.: Wayne Gretzky, Sidney Crosby, and More*. Minneapolis: Lerner Publications, 2020.

NHL
https://www.nhl.com/

Sports Illustrated Kids—Hockey
https://www.sikids.com/hockey

Storden, Thom. *Hockey's Greatest Game-Winning Goals and Other Crunch-Time Heroics*. New York: Sports Illustrated Kids, 2020.

INDEX

PHOTO ACKNOWLEDGMENTS

Image credits: Craig Melvin/Stringer/Getty Images, p.4; Craig Melvin/Stringer/Getty Images, p.5; Graig Abel/Contributo/Getty Images, p.6; Andre Ringuette/Contributor/Getty Images, p.7; Harry How/Staff/Getty Images, p.8; Jamie Squire/Staff/Getty Images, p.9; Focus On Sport/Contributor/Getty Images, p.10; Focus On Sport/Contributor/Getty Images, p.11; B Bennett/Contributor/Getty Images, p.12; B Miller/Contributor/Getty Images, p.13; Denis Brodeur/Contributor/Getty Images, p.14; Steve Babineau/Contributor/Getty Images, p.15; Bruce Bennett/Contributor/Getty Images, p.16; B Bennett/Contributor/Getty Images, p.17; Bob Olsen/Contributor/Getty Images, p.18; Bettmann/Contributor/Getty Images, p.19; Denis Brodeur/Contributor/Getty Images, p.20; B Bennett/Contributor/Getty Images, p.21; Jed Jacobsohn/Staff/Getty Images, p.22; Nevin Reid/Stringer/Getty Images, 23; Dave Reginek/Contributor/Getty Images, p.24; Dave Sandford/Contributor/Getty Images, p.25; Andy Marlin/Contributor/Getty Images, p.26; Mitchell Layton/Contributor/Getty Images, p.27

Cover: Dave Sandford/Stringer/Getty Images; Norm Hall/Contributor/Getty Images; Doug Pensinger/Staff/Getty Images